Oxford
International
Resources

2

Activity Book

T0355070

Deborah Roberts
Shahbano Bilgrami
Liz Gibbs

OXFORD
UNIVERSITY PRESS

Contents

Homes

In this topic, learners are encouraged to:

- recognize shapes and describe them
- learn about different building materials
- discover different homes from around the world
- make simple comparisons
- talk about animals and their homes
- discuss why animals and people need homes.

Teachers will also help learners to:

- talk about changes in their own lives
- practise tracing letters and numbers
- identify and use rhyming words
- think about the connection between weather and building materials
- explore fiction and non-fiction texts.

Homes for everyone

a Find the home you like best.

b Look. How are the houses different?

c Listen to your teacher and find the shapes.

d Find Hoppy's friend.

At home

Walk near to your house and find different buildings. Ask your child to describe the shapes of windows and doors.

In these sessions, children will also: compare homes with their own, review familiar shapes, draw their home, design a new home, find out how houses are made. → TG pp. 60–63

a Count the workers.

b Find the tools and the materials.

In this session, children will also: learn about different building materials, act out construction jobs, build houses with blocks, talk about homes in stories. → TG pp. 60–63

At home

Help your child describe your home. Ask: *How many (bedrooms) do we have? What materials can you see?*

Homes for everyone

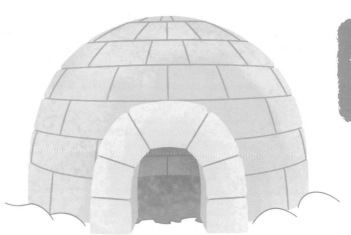

a Listen to your teacher and count the things you can see.

b Compare the houses.

At home

Take a walk with your child, looking at all the different homes. Ask: *How many different materials can you see being used?*

In this session, children will also: talk about the features of different houses, make a street of model houses, count in sets of 6. → TG pp. 60–63

7

Connect

a Draw lines to match the walls with the materials.

b Draw a pattern of bricks on the wall.

c Colour Humpty Dumpty.

At home

Count the number of walls in different rooms with your child. Ask: *What colour are they?*

In this session, children will also: sing songs and rhymes and play games about walls, look at walls and brick patterns, learn about materials for building walls. → TG pp. 60–63

My home

Moving day

a Look and say how Sam feels **before** and **after** moving.

b Retell the story.

At home
Build a cosy little 'home' with your child using sheets, chairs, and cushions.

In this session, children will also: sing a song, talk about their memories and feelings, practice counting to 10. → TG pp. 63–66

Explore

a Sing Moving day.

b Trace the line to help Sam get to his new home.

c Count the trees Sam passes on his way.

At home

Set out a tray of rock salt or shaving cream. Encourage your child to use their finger to trace different patterns in it: straight lines, zigzags, swirls.

In this session, children will also: create a map, listen to instructions and follow a route on a map, use a pencil with good control. → TG pp. 63–66

a Trace the shapes with a pencil.

b Draw lines to match the objects with their shapes.

At home

Explore rooms at home with your child. Ask what makes them soft or comfortable. Then name a shape and ask your child to find an object with that shape.

In this session, children will also: identify 2D shapes, describe fabric colours and textures, design the inside of a room. → TG pp. 63–66

a Listen to your teacher and draw your home.

In this session, children will also: sing a new verse of the song, compare their home to others, make sets of 7 objects. → TG pp. 63–66

At home

Go with your child outside your home. Ask: *What shapes and colours can you see? Is the roof flat or does it slope?*

My home

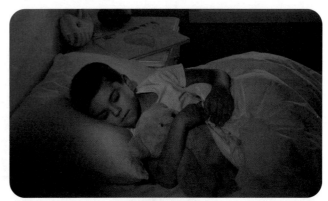

a Look and say which room each picture shows.

b Draw your favourite room at home.

In this session, children will also: count and identify rooms in houses, link activities to different rooms, talk about happy times at home. → TG pp. 63–66

At home

Ask your child about what they enjoy doing at home and in which rooms.

Building homes

3

a Practise the Building rhyme.

b Find the different materials for the houses.

c Look. Are the houses flat or curved?

d Find the construction toys.

At home

Build two houses with your child: one out of building bricks, the other out of card. Test to see which is stronger by putting a weight on them.

In these sessions, children will also: talk about construction and building materials, make model huts or log cabins, play a game using rhyming words. → TG pp. 67–69

brick

metal

a Trace the letters with a pencil.

b Count the windows and doors.

At home

Discuss with your child how homes protect us from the weather. For example, in hot places, homes keep us cool. In cold places, homes keep us warm.

In this session, children will also: compare building materials, find out that metal objects get hot or cold, make a model brick house. → TG pp. 67–69

Building homes

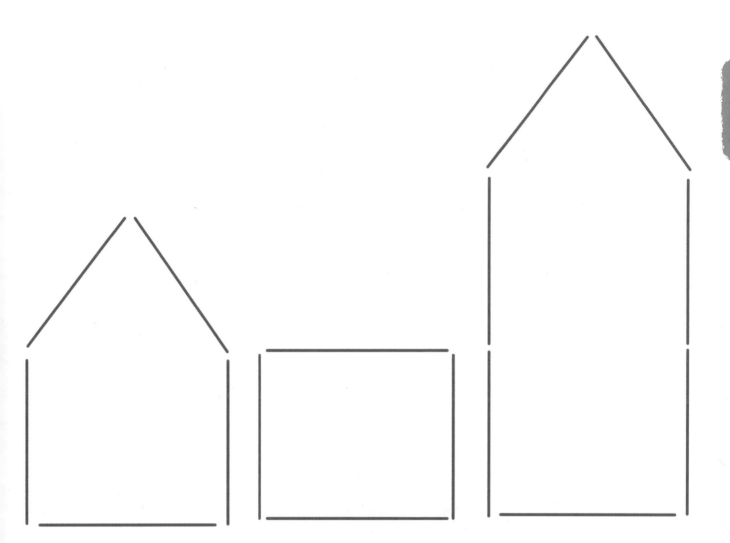

_____   _____   _____

a Circle the slopes.

b Number the houses 1 to 3 from the
shortest to the tallest.

At home

Help your child
choose materials to make
a house. Encourage them
to describe its parts using
words such as *tall*, *short*,
narrow, *wide*.

In this session, children will also: make simple comparisons (tallest, shortest, biggest), explore
the way water moves, test materials for a waterproof roof. → TG pp. 67–69

17

Building homes

a Draw lines to match the houses with the weather.

In this session, children will also: find out about homes in hot and cold places, talk about their homes, count sounds. → TG pp. 67–69

Animal homes

a Sing Animal homes.

b Find the animal homes.

c Count the fish in the pond.

d Look. Which animals fly?

At home

With your child, explore your garden or the local park for animal homes. You can take photos.

In this session, children will also: identify animal homes and find out their names, go for a nature walk, practise sorting and counting toy animals. → TG pp. 70–72

Animal homes

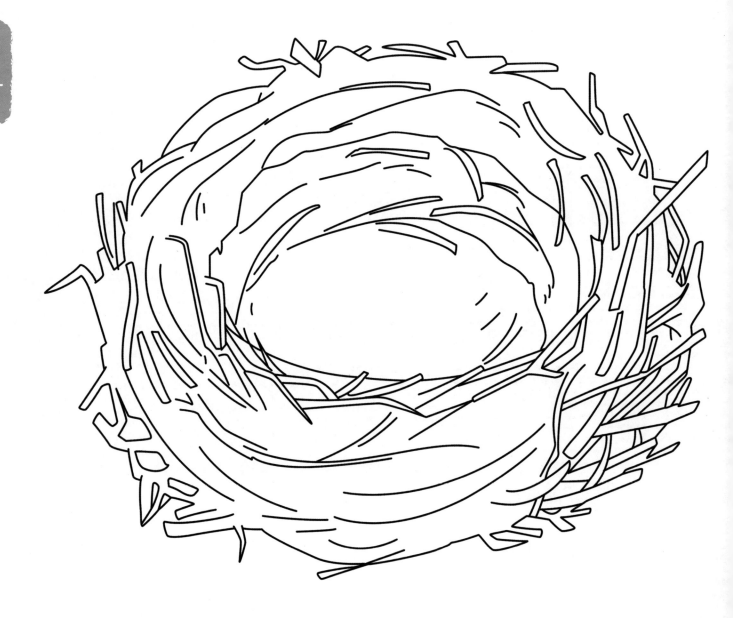

a Draw some mice in the nest.

b Count the mice in your picture.

In this session, children will also: find out about different animal nests, make nests with natural materials, sing animal rhymes and songs. → TG pp. 70–72

At home

Talk about any animals or pets you see when with your child. Ask: *Where does it sleep at night?*

Animal homes

a Look. What is the same about these homes?

2   3

7   8

b Count the rabbits **above** the ground.
Count the rabbits **below** the ground.

c Trace the correct numbers.

In this session, children will also: find out about underground homes, write numbers 0–9, explore tunnels. → TG pp. 70–72

a Count the animals in each picture.
Which pictures have the same number
of animals?

b Say the total number of animals.

In this session, children will also: find out about animal dens, act out a story, count sets and find totals, make rhyming words. → TG pp. 70–72

Animal homes

a Find the homes.

b Draw lines to match the homes with the animals.

At home

Ask: *Where do different animals live? What do animals need to help them stay happy, warm, and safe?* Compare these needs to ours.

In this session, children will also: review their learning by talking about why animals and people need homes, making a model home, saying rhyming words. → TG pp. 70–72

Food

In this topic, learners are encouraged to:

- talk about foods and preferences
- think about foods they enjoy in different weather
- name ingredients and put recipe steps in order
- describe flavours and identify foods from other countries
- use numbers to count items in a set
- talk about food and its journey to our tables.

Teachers will also help learners to:

- talk about a celebration they have attended
- review shapes
- discuss healthy choices in food
- take part in games and races
- learn about cooking as a way to process food
- say numbers 1 to 10 in order and practise counting.

Party food

a Look. What is Fiona doing?

b Find the book.

c Name the foods.

d Sing Cooking is fun.

In this session, children will also: talk about making food, remember a party they have been to, design party invitations. → TG pp. 73–76

At home
Help your child write down 3 'Cooking rules'. Use simple pictures to illustrate them. Hang this up in your kitchen.

Party food

a Look. What is happening?

b Find the foods and drinks that are best for a hot day.

c Draw the foods and drinks you like.

In this session, children will also: notice signs outside that tell them about the weather, talk about food for hot or cold days, make party hats. → TG pp. 73–76

At home

Talk about foods your child likes to eat when it is hot and when it is cold. Why are some foods better for hot weather and others for cold weather?

Party food

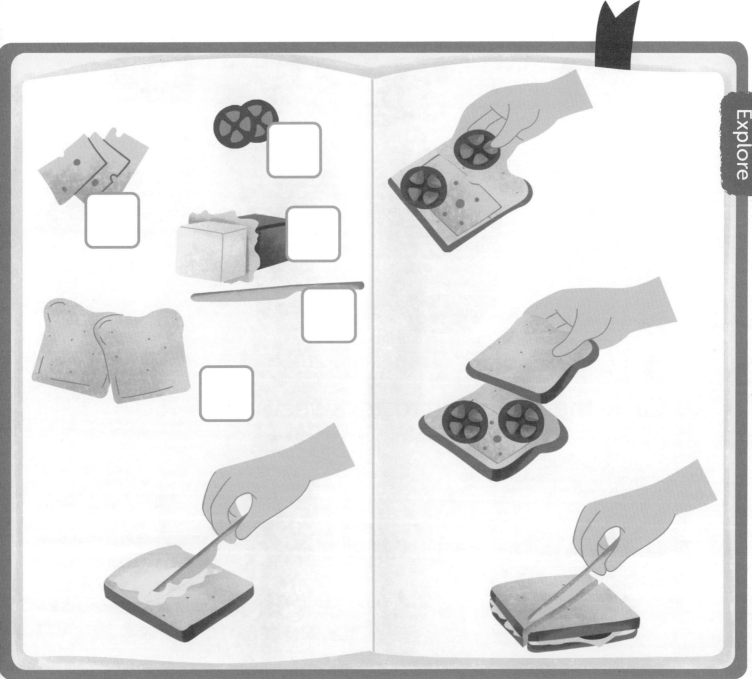

a Tick (✓) the ingredients.

b Look at the recipe.
Find the first step in the recipe.

In this session, children will also: read recipes, learn what ingredients are, put recipe steps in order, make their own sandwiches. → TG pp. 73–76

At
home
Help your child make
a sandwich to eat.

a Circle the filling that tastes sweet.

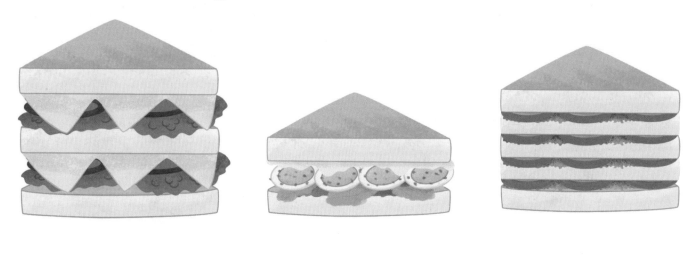

_____   _____   _____

b Look at the 3 sandwiches.
What do you think is in them?

c Number the sandwiches 1 to 3 from
the smallest to the biggest.

At home

Talk about different
sandwich fillings. Encourage
your child to try a sandwich
with a filling that they have
not tried before.

In this session, children will also: describe tastes and textures, make simple comparisons,
make modelling clay 'sandwiches', taste and vote for their favourite filling. → TG pp. 73–76

Party food

a Name the party foods.
How many are there?

b Tick (✓) the sweet foods.

c Circle the healthy foods.

In this session, children will also: talk about party food, sort sweet treats and healthy food, get ready for a party, welcome guests to their party. → TG pp. 73–76

At home

Try out a simple recipe
with your child.
Allow them to help you
measure and mix.

Picnic food

a Look. What are the children doing?

b Say the Teddy bears' picnic rhyme.

c Find Maya's teddy bear.

d Count the ants.

At home

Help your child use the words *under*, *on top*, *behind*, and *in front* to describe where objects and toys are in your home.

In these sessions, children will also: count sets of objects, use prepositions in play, learn how eggs change when boiled, design a class picnic blanket. → TG pp. 77–79

Picnic food

a Look. Count the colours.

b Name the fruits you know.

c Draw more fruit on the fruit kebab.

In this session, children will also: talk about ingredients, make a fruit kebab, review properties of shapes, find out about picnic foods around the world. → TG pp. 77–79

At home

Help your child make a fruit kebab or fruit salad. Encourage them to name the fruits and describe their colour, shape, and taste.

Picnic food

a Look at the jumbled pictures. Find something oval.

b Order the pictures 1 to 5.

In this session, children will also: say a rhyme, learn how to make a frittata, count to 10, make model food. → TG pp. 77–79

At home

When cooking with your child, talk about what you are doing. Use words such as *first*, *next*, *then*, and *finally*.

33

Picnic food

Connect

a Circle the picnic.

b Look. What are the children in the race doing?

In this session, children will also: talk about hurting others' feelings and saying sorry, try balancing objects on a spoon, have a teddy bears' picnic, make a recipe book. → TG pp. 77–79

World food

Rani's rice pudding

1

2

3

4

a Look. Who is helping Rani?

b Find Rani looking sad.

c Retell the story.

At home

Talk with your child about a time when you had a special family meal. What did you eat? Who was there?

In this session, children will also: talk about cooking at home, look at world recipe books, compare 'full' and 'empty'. → TG pp. 80–82

35

World food

a Look at the children's food.
Count how many on each plate.

b Look at the shapes.
What are their names?

c Draw lines to match the foods with
their shapes.

At home

Show your child how
to wash their hands
before touching food.
Let them help you make
a special family recipe.

In this session, children will also: find out about different food, try new food, describe the
taste, share a story about cooking, sing 'Five currant buns'. → TG pp. 80–82

World food

a Count the toppings.

b Look. Tick (✓) the toppings for Mexican sopes.

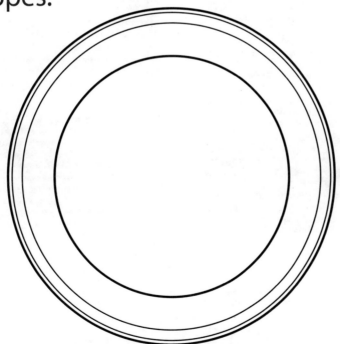

c Draw toppings for your sope.

In this session, children will also: learn about Mexican sopes (stuffed corn cakes), watch another dish being made, make a model of a sope, compare 'more' and 'less'. → TG pp. 80–82

At home

Ask your child about some of their favourite foods. Do any of them come from another part of the world?

World food

Explore

a Find the tree. What fruit is it?

b Say how the fruit went from the tree to the girl's home.

At home

Talk with your child about the fruit and vegetables they eat, and where these have come from.

In this session, children will also: find out about food journeys, act out an apple's journey, find out where some fruit comes from, compare 'more' and 'less'. → TG pp. 80–82

World food

a Circle 5 foods for a party or picnic.

b Choose 1 food and say how to make it.

In this session, children will: review their learning by describing a recipe, sharing 10 in different ways, painting and talking about favourite foods, singing songs and rhymes. → TG pp. 80–82

At home

Ask your child what food they would like to share with family and friends for a celebration.

Weather and seasons

In this topic, learners are encouraged to:

- recognize weather elements and their effects
- describe the seasons
- name clothes useful for different seasons
- count from 1 to 10, sets, and the total number of objects
- explore the lifecycle of fruit
- learn about animals that hatch from eggs.

Teachers will also help learners to:

- join in with rhymes, songs, and poems
- participate in role-plays
- observe the natural world and learn about plants and animals
- look for evidence of seasonal change.

All kinds of weather

a Look. What is happening?

b Find something made of sand.

c Count the swimmers.

d Look again. Who looks happy?

At home

Talk about today's weather with your child. How does it make them feel?

41

In these sessions, children will also: use a weather chart, listen to stories, make objects move, count and compare objects by size, make a wind sock. → TG pp. 84–86

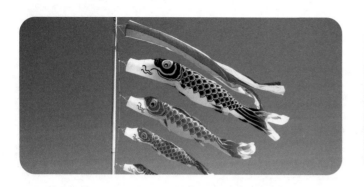

a Look. What is making these things move?

pull   push

b Trace the letters.

c Look. What is each child doing?

In this session, children will also: find out what the wind can do, investigate pushing and pulling, practice writing letter 'p', make flags. → TG pp. 84–86

At home

Provide opportunities for your child to push and pull different things and see how the objects move.

Explore

All kinds of weather

a Circle the glass that is half full.

b Listen to your teacher and colour the water in the glasses.

In this session, children will also: find out about staying safe in the sun, compare cups that are full, empty and half full. → TG pp. 84–86

All kinds of weather

a Listen to your teacher and find the activities.

b Draw lines to match the shadows with the objects.

At home

Talk with your child about how much water they drink in a day. Ask: *Why is it important to drink water?*

In this session, children will also: identify objects linked to safety in the sun, talk about favourite activities in the sun, practise listening carefully, investigate shadows. → TG pp. 84–86

Changing seasons

a Look. What is Ms Zara teaching?

b Find the tree in winter.

c Look at Sam. What is the matter?

d Count Maya's leaves.

At home

Go on a walk with your child and collect items to show what season it is, such as flowers and leaves.

In this session, children will also: talk about weather and seasons, learn a seasons rhyme, think about feelings, remember clothes they have worn. → TG pp. 87–90

Changing seasons

a Count the apple seeds aloud.

b Order the pictures 1 to 4.

At home

Allow your child to explore different fruits with seeds. Help them compare the number of seeds in each.

In this session, children will also: learn about the life cycle of fruit, count seeds, plant seeds, paint trees to show seasonal changes. → TG pp. 87–90

Changing seasons

a Look. What season is it?

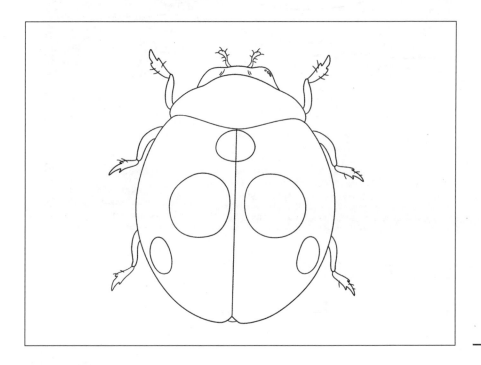

b Colour your ladybird.
Write how many spots you coloured.

At home

Go outside together and look for signs of the season. Look at the weather, trees, leaves, fruit, and flowers.

47

Changing seasons

a Look. What season is it? Why?

b Colour the smallest items ❄ and the biggest items ❄.

c Choose a colour and colour the medium-sized items.

In this session, children will also: imagine a scene, retell a traditional story, talk about a character's feelings, order items by size. → TG pp. 87–90

At home
Encourage your child to order everyday objects from smallest to largest and largest to smallest.

Changing seasons

a Name the seasons. Which one is missing?

b Choose a season. Find something you might wear in this season.

In this session, children will also: choose clothes for different types of weather, make repeating patterns, make groups of 2–5. → TG pp. 87–90

At home

Talk with your child about clothes that are useful for each season. Ask: *When would you wear a woolly hat?*

Springtime

a Look. Where are the children?

b Count the eggs in the basket.

c Sing and dance to Waddle, waddle, quack, quack.

d Find the chicks hatching.

At home

Play 'odd one out' by showing your child similar objects with one completely unrelated object. Ask them to find the 'odd one out'.

In these sessions, children will also: hear and retell the story of the 'Ugly Duckling', compare egg sizes, spot the odd one out, find out about hatching eggs. → TG pp. 90–93

Springtime

a Circle the items you can find in nature.

b Look. Where can you find the other items?

In this session, children will also: go for a nature walk, sort objects from nature and things that are made by people, review basic shapes. → TG pp. 90–93

At home

Find different objects at home. Ask your child which objects are natural and which aren't.

Springtime

a Look at the eggs. What colour are they?

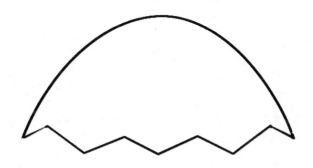

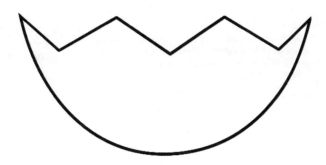

b Draw and colour a baby animal hatching from the egg.

In this session, children will also: learn about other animals that hatch from eggs, play a guessing game, sing songs about animals. → TG pp. 90–93

At home

Talk with your child about some of the animals that hatch from eggs, such as birds, snakes, and lizards. Can you find pictures of any of these animals hatching?

Springtime

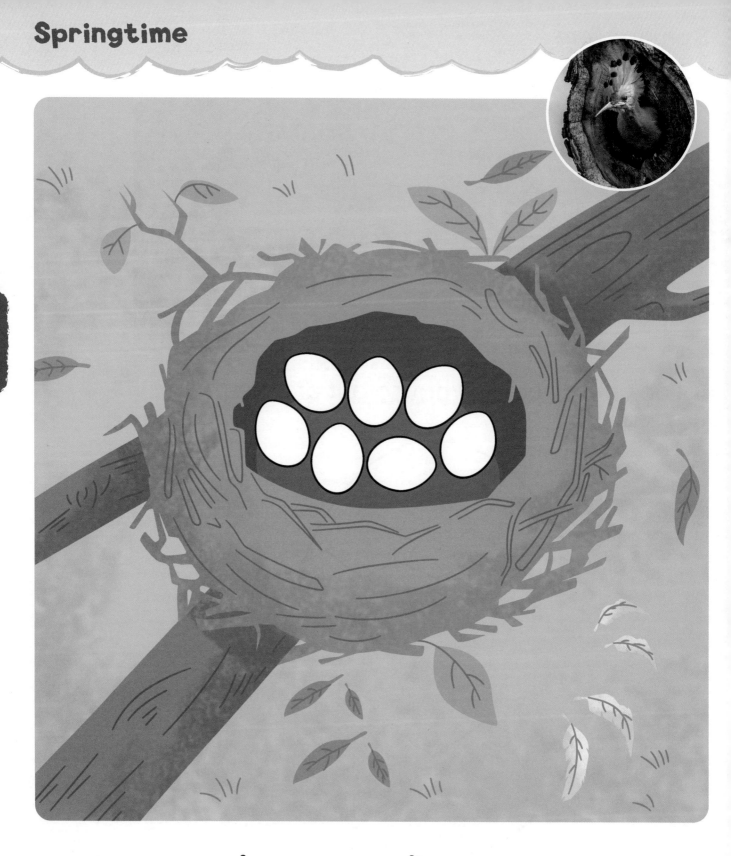

a Colour 3 eggs 🌑 and 2 eggs 🌑. Draw small spots on the white eggs.

b How many eggs are there in total?

In this session, children will also: compare numbers using less and more, talk about being safe and cared for, review the sequence of egg hatching. → TG pp. 90–93

At home

Look at a picture of a bird's nest with your child. Can your child describe it? Ask why animal homes need to be safe.

Connect

Rain! Rain!

a Look. What is the weather like?

b How are the children feeling?

In this session, children will also: talk about sheltering from the weather, describe feelings, make weather observations, play a jumping game. → TG pp. 94–96

Rain! Rain!

a Look. How many raindrops are falling from each cloud?

b Draw more raindrops so that all the clouds have the same.

In this session, children will also: make raindrops as they play, share stories and information about rain. → TG pp. 94–96

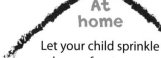

At home

Let your child sprinkle drops of water on a waterproof coat. What do they notice?

Rain! Rain!

a Look. What sounds might the children hear in each picture?

b Finish drawing and colouring the pictures.

In this session, children will also: listen to and describe weather sounds, make weather sounds in different ways, make a rainstick, count sounds. → TG pp. 94–96

At home

If your child is frightened of thunder, talk about ways of feeling better, such as having a hug or reading a story.

Rain! Rain!

Wednesday	Thursday	Friday
☀	🌧	☀

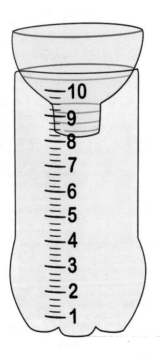
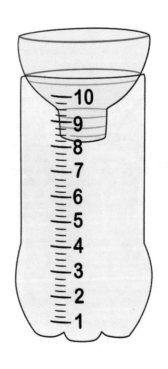
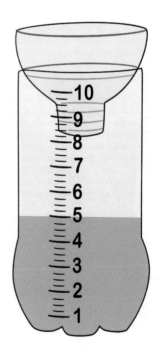

a Circle the gauge that has rainwater in it.

b Draw a line from that gauge to the day when it rained.

At home

Help your child record the morning weather on a chart for 5 days. Can they see any patterns?

In this session, children will also: observe the weather, compare and order rain gauges with water in them, paint rainy day pictures, make weather pointers. → TG pp. 94–96

Rain! Rain!

a Draw lines to match the umbrellas that are the same.

b Circle the umbrella that is different.

At home

On a rainy day, encourage your child to practise writing on steamy windows. They can write their name or letters they know.

a Look. What is happening outside?

b Count the books.

c Listen to your teacher and clap out the rhythms of each poem.

d Say which poem you like best.

At home

Help your child tap out the rhythm of their favourite nursery rhymes using pots and wooden spoons.

In these sessions, children will listen to and join in with poems and rhymes, play rhyming word games, make snowflakes. → TG pp. 97–99

I can hear it!

Explore

a Look. How many things can you name?

b Listen to your teacher and circle the sounds that rhyme with *ice*.

At home

Add ice cubes to a transparent glass of water. Help your child notice what happens when the ice cubes melt.

62 In this session, children will also: practise hearing rhyming words, find out about winter weather, watch ice melt, compare 'bigger' and 'smaller'. → TG pp. 97–99

I can hear it!

a Look. What is the weather like in each picture?

b Colour and count the jewels.

In this session, children will also: make up rhymes about stormy weather, count sets and make groups of different sizes, complete an obstacle course. → TG pp. 97–99

At home

Use picture books or photos to show your child different kinds of boats and ships. You can explain how they move.

I can hear it!

a Look at each tree. What is the weather like in each season?

b Complete the pictures.

In this session, children will also: review their learning about seasons and clothing for different weather, comparing numbers using 'less' and 'more', ordering a set of objects by size. → TG pp. 97–99

At home

Ask your child to choose their favourite song or rhyme from this week. Encourage them to sing or say it.